THE LISTENING SKILLS POCKETBOOK

Mike Pezet

Drawings by Phil Hailstone

Published by:
Management Pocketbooks Ltd
Wild's Yard, The Dean, Alresford, Hants, SO24 9BQ, U.K.
Tel: +44 (0)1962 735573   Fax: +44 (0)1962 733637
Email: sales@pocketbook.co.uk
Website: www.pocketbook.co.uk

© Mike Pezet 2018

This edition published 2018
ISBN 978 1 910186 03 9
E-book ISBN 978 1 907078 75 0

British Library Cataloguing-in-Publication Data – A catalogue record for this book is available from the British Library.

Design, typesetting and graphics by **zpek ltd.**   Printed in U.K.

CONTENTS

To Jess, Louis and Erin.
Each of you inspire in your own unique way.

INTRODUCTION

COMMON SCENARIOS

How often have you encountered the following scenario?

You are talking with your manager, colleague or friend and a tiny light flashes. You see his head tilt, his eyes shift, his body incline towards his phone. The shift in his attention is visible.

Perhaps on this occasion it simply washed over you because it happens all the time, but perhaps you were on the point of saying something important and then stopped. Perhaps you felt insignificant, part of the furniture.

What if he had 'managed the moment', ignored the phone, focused on you? What impression would that have created?

COMMON SCENARIOS

What about this scenario? You're highlighting a potential issue to your line manager; something you consider important: looming deadlines, for example, or conflicting priorities.

Suddenly you're no longer resolving your issue. For some reason the conversation has switched to your manager's woes; you hear that you *'don't have to deal with what I deal with'* or *'you should see **my** workload'*, and more of the same.

Maybe she really did have more important things to attend to and your issue didn't warrant much attention. But maybe it could have been resolved on the spot in a brief conversation.

Maybe you left confused, wondering <u>how</u> the conversation had shifted. It made you think of her as self-absorbed and you may hesitate to talk to her next time there is a problem, thinking *'why bother?'* You might even begin to think 'management' in general aren't interested.

INTRODUCTION

COMMON SCENARIOS

It is easy to dismiss these small daily encounters as insignificant. If you don't need to work with others to achieve success then you can do just that. If you don't need to influence people constructively, be they senior, junior or equal to you, you can easily make light of such experiences.

On the other hand, if you think success at work comes from a productive relationship between yourself and others, then listening helps make that relationship successful. Listening is the foundation stone. If you think influence depends on understanding other people's needs and desires, then listening helps you know, rather than guess, those needs. **Listening is momentary, its effects are not.**

For you, for those you work with and for your organisation, listening has short- and long-term benefits. On the following pages we will look at some of them.

BENEFITS OF LISTENING

Personal and one-to-one benefits	Organisational benefits
Trust Listening is integral in the formation and maintenance of trust	People are more open and share more with leaders they feel listen to them, giving leaders more insight into the organisation
Feedback People are less likely to reject feedback if they feel listened to and are less defensive when feeling threatened	Generative feedback is important to personal and organisational development
Relationships Listening affects the nature and quality of relationships	The quality of relationship between manager and employee affects a wide range of outcomes, eg: engagement, adaptability to change, desire to remain in or leave the organisation

INTRODUCTION

BENEFITS OF LISTENING

Personal and one-to-one benefits	Organisational benefits
Difference Listening enables you to hear and begin to understand, even appreciate, different styles and perceptions	Different approaches can be a catalyst for innovation. If people believe they're not listened to, creativity is stifled
Openness It reduces the potential for people to defend and become entrenched in a position	Leaders can gain deeper insights into the causes of resistance to change
Relationships Listening plays an important role in helping people through change. A manager can understand where people are in the stages of change, eg precontemplation, etc	Positive responses to change correlate to satisfaction with managerial communication

BENEFITS OF LISTENING

Personal and one-to-one benefits	Organisational benefits
Conflict Listening can help de-escalate conflict and help people find solutions	Constructive conflict can be a productive catalyst for solutions and innovation
Creativity It can create the conditions where people willingly offer ideas, solutions, etc	Involving people in strategy formulation generates new options and commitment
Communication Listening effectively can reduce the potential for misunderstanding	Misunderstandings can cause project overruns, costs, missed opportunities
Respect Listening effectively makes people feel respected and valued	People who feel respected and valued by the organisation can convey positive attitudes to customers

With so many benefits from something simple like listening you wonder how so many people get it so wrong?

GETTING IT WRONG

You'll be good at spotting a 'bad' listener but you may not be as good at recognising when you're the bad listener. Why? Here are some of the main reasons:

Personal factors
- Listening is habitual, taken for granted and operates on the periphery of consciousness, therefore it is hard to monitor yourself *in the moment*
- People are born problem-solvers with a propensity to leap to offering solutions before hearing all the story
- Many people feel uncomfortable with silence and feel compelled to speak when a pause would be more powerful
- Many are convinced their view is right, if only the *other* person would listen

Structural factors
- People have numerous competing demands on their time and attention
- Power influences the value placed on listening to someone with less power

What would your colleagues say about the quality of your listening?

YOUR MOTIVATION FOR LISTENING

What is your motivation for developing your listening? Some people seem to be naturally good listeners but most need to learn how to improve. Anyone in the 'helping' professions such as counselling, psychology or coaching must learn to manage listening because it is intrinsic to the profession.

What about you? If you're not in a helping profession and your listening is 'good enough', why bother developing it now? Perhaps you want:

- To be more successful in your role by engaging others
- To address some feedback you've received about your listening or impact on others
- To help others develop their capability
- To better understand others' motivations or priorities
- To manage upwards more effectively by understanding your boss's priorities better
- To get a stronger connection with colleagues, friends or family

Perhaps one or two of those caught your attention. Perhaps you're attracted by the benefits of being a better listener. If so, read on.

WHO THE BOOK IS FOR

Managers – Anyone needing to achieve success through others. Developing your listening can help you understand the barriers and enablers to their performance.

Leaders – Leadership is about engaging emotions and how you listen strikes people at emotional levels.

SME/entrepreneurs – owner-managers growing their business can be caught between passion for their idea and juggling multiple hats. You can lose sight of what engages your most precious asset: your staff, the knowledge they have built and their motivation to use it.

Manager coaches or coaches in general – for anyone embarking on a coaching journey listening is the bedrock. Without good listening good questions are left to chance.

Trainers – you will gain insight into factors that enable and hinder effective listening.

Anyone interested in better interactions – listening has a subtle yet profound effect on interactions with colleagues, family and friends. A small change can make a big difference.

WHAT THE BOOK OFFERS

Not every situation requires good listening. Time wouldn't allow it and you would burn out, so the book doesn't advocate continual high-level listening.

Listening with purpose **varies**, depending on your role and context. Someone in customer services will listen for different things from a focus group interviewer or a teacher.

In the book, we don't look at ways to listen in each and every context; there isn't space. The important lesson is to become aware that in any situation you might just need to move up a gear, and change how you listen.

WHAT THE BOOK OFFERS

The aim, therefore, is to put you in the driver's seat of your listening. To give you tools to recognise when and how someone could benefit from great listening and the steps you can take to deliver it.

The challenge to alter deep-seated habits is not to be underestimated. To help you, the book will outline what gets in the way of something as simple and impactful as listening. How habits built over a lifetime shape your perception, which in turn influences how you listen and who you're listening to.

You will find some straightforward, easy-to-apply tools to help you develop listening skills, skills that will stand you in good stead across situations such as conflict, influencing or everyday engagement. Listening is only one side of the equation because the quality of your listening is demonstrated in your response. We look at some structures for responding.

The outcome is to be **effective** and **impactful** through being in control of how you listen and respond.

INTERFERENCES

OVERVIEW

Before satellite and mobile technology, the world relied on radio communication. Between a radio transmitter and a receiver many things interfered with a message. Storms cut signals, atmospherics distorted messages, transmissions were weakened. The original broadcast might contain errors or signals were lost through faulty equipment or operator skill.

It's the same with communication between people. All manner of things interfere with hearing because even though we live in a digital world we still communicate verbally, as we've done since the dawn of time.

This chapter looks at some of the main interferences and what you can do about them. They range from obvious things like your immediate environment, through to structural factors like the effect of power and how perception and the way you've learnt to listen affect what you pay attention to and hear.

ENVIRONMENTAL FACTORS

The most obvious interference with listening is the surrounding environment. Environmental distractions are numerous; some are obvious and manageable whilst others are obscure but influential.

HMMMM!

CRASH!

Background noise such as talking, the hubbub of an open plan office or noise from traffic or construction are obvious. They're interferences that can cause you only partly to hear what is said. Surprisingly, many people tolerate the noise, don't change the situation, and don't fully hear, losing some of what was meant.

BEEP BEEP!

BANG!

Yet the solution is simple. Firstly, notice the interference then take responsibility to change the situation. It is okay to interrupt the flow of conversation. If you change the location you'll change the hearing.

RING RING!

19

ENVIRONMENTAL FACTORS

Another interference is communication style. Someone's pace, tone, words and observations, could be fast, slow, rambling, logical, creative or expressed in their second language. You may find it hard to follow and understand, but yet you act like you are listening by nodding, smiling and making eye contact.

Maintaining the façade may seem less awkward than stopping and managing the situation. Many people feel too embarrassed to do this. Perhaps they worry that revealing any fallibility will damage their credibility, or they don't want to upset the other person. Which is more honest and respectful? The façade or wanting to do something about it?

Again, the solution is simple: take responsibility and manage the moment. Try accepting it isn't anyone's fault. Try telling the person you want to hear them fully, that it is your issue not theirs. Guide them with how they might help you, eg, *'I want to hear properly. Could you – slow the pace for me', 'simplify the language for me', 'bear with me if I ask you to repeat',* etc.

 The choice to manage the moment, to take responsibility is yours.

CULTURE

Highly influential but difficult to see are the cultural norms surrounding you. The value society places on listening, for instance. In western cultures listening is looked on as passive, lower status, less powerful than speaking. Advocating, pushing strong opinions is considered powerful, influential. Authority speaks – you should listen.

Yet in other cultures listening is seen as influential. It enables important information to be gleaned from the speaker, it enables speakers to be heard and witnessed, to feel powerful. It enables questions or statements of relevance and precision to be formed, which can stimulate thought and insight.

Culture is difficult to see and shapes people's behaviour in society, organisations and teams. To change the patterns you need to identify them and ask, *'Does it always have to be this way? Aren't there alternative ways of acting that would be more effective?'*

POWER

Power is interesting in relation to listening, specifically the dynamic of power.

Power means being able to direct or influence people or the course of events. Power lies in access to information, resources and networks of people. You employ power by combining some or all of the authority people think you have; the reward or punishment they think you can give; your expertise and your personality, ie charisma.

One dynamic of power is to over- and underestimate your abilities. As power grows it is easy to overestimate your competence, your wisdom, the control you have and expertise in areas you know little about.

If, on the other hand, you perceive you have low power, you can underestimate your ability to influence or be heard. You are reluctant to question or challenge because you anticipate consequences, such as loss of access to rewards or influence.

Because people socialise with those of similar status the dynamics tend to be self-reinforcing, further embedding beliefs and perceptions.

POWER GAPS

So what does power have to do with listening? There are a number of considerations:

- The self-reinforcing nature of the dynamic can increase the power gap. Those with power become more convinced of their 'rightness' and only hear what they want to hear

- Those less powerful become more convinced of their powerlessness and retreat into silence

- When people are less senior they spend a lot of time listening to others. As they assume positions of authority they spend more time being listened to

- The conviction and reinforcement of their personal superiority can lead to discounting others' opinions, particularly if counter to their views

- Large power gaps are not healthy. IBM, RBS, unchecked film moguls and stars, to name a few, provide examples of some of the problems caused by unchecked power exaggerating someone's sense of their own importance

The answer? Be mindful of the effects of power. Be aware that your self-belief, particularly regarding your own importance, specialness or superiority to others, affects how you hear and the impact you have. Appreciate others' situations and perspectives; listen with an open mind.

INTERFERENCES

YOU

The most challenging interference with your listening is you yourself.

One reason is that your listening is automatic. You've grown up developing habits that help you listen with a minimum of fuss and effort, and filter and shape **how** you listen. Think of them as autopilots.

Another reason is that you aren't taught to listen. School tells you to listen but doesn't teach you how to do so. Throughout your career your good and bad autopilots are embedded further.

Some careers, however, require old habits to be undone: coaches, counsellors, the police, for example, are trained to listen. They understand that effective listening doesn't just 'happen'. They know they need to make a conscious choice to listen, to switch off the autopilot.

They know that just because they can hear doesn't mean they are listening.

IT'S HARD TO BE YOUR OWN CRITIC

Recognising that you interfere with how and what you hear is not easy because it's not obvious to you that you aren't listening effectively. Your focus and attention may be more on hearing your own thoughts and concerns than you realise.

Unless people actually tell you *'you're not listening to me'* you'll generally be oblivious to how well you are listening. If misunderstandings arise the typical tactic is to blame the other person, which is great because you're not at fault and don't need to change.

Great listeners recognise that their listening influences outcomes and the development of relationships, and that effective listening takes effort.

LUNCH?

PERCEPTION

The perceptions you have of others also interfere with your listening. The Arbinger Institute book *'Leadership and Self-deception'* explores how the way you perceive other people legitimises how you treat and relate to them.

In broad terms your perception 'boxes' people into:

- **Objects** – you minimise people's needs, ideas, qualities, emotions. **Your** needs are of more value and importance and you can excuse your own behaviour. You can see this in action on trains. Watch people elevate the status of their bag to stop others sitting next to them, people who have all sorts of needs

- **Subjects** – you recognise other people's needs, aspirations, ideas and emotions as valid and of equal worth to your own. You recognise that negotiation and compromise are important for productive relationships

A consequence of power is to view those on the other side of a power gap as objects, losing you a source of creativity and innovation. One perception requires minimal effort, the other effort and engagement. View people as objects and you're not listening to a person, you're listening to a stereotype.

SUBJECTS NOT OBJECTS

Take this example of Josh, a manager on a modular residential leadership programme.

> At the start of the programme people shared their development goals. Josh categorically stated: *'to find out how to get rid of the worst and most time-consuming performer in my team. I waste endless time trying to manage Scot'*.
>
> During the course Josh received all kinds of advice from his peers but remained adamant the person was *'a write off'*. The programme closed with workshops on perceptions and coaching skills such as questioning and listening.
>
> At the three-month development review everyone was curious about Josh's situation. Reporting developments, he humbly said, *'Well ... actually, Scot is now my star performer and I would hate to lose him. I decided to try a different frame of mind and actually listen to what he wanted. I understood him and what he wants better. Now I work differently with him and can't hold him back'*.

Josh's shift to seeing Scot as a person (subject) not an object brought about a change in how he listened, which in turn brought out unnoticed qualities.

REACTING TO CHALLENGING INFORMATION

Another factor that gets in the way of hearing someone is your reaction to information that challenges you. The information could be bad news or something that challenges your values or expectations. If they are telling you something that shocks you, your reaction will block your ability to engage with the content of the communication.

Typically, the reaction follows a trajectory:

- Surprise, shock or disbelief
- Resistance, denial, denigration
- Secondary thinking, accommodation
- Acceptance, negotiation, change

REACTING TO CHALLENGING INFORMATION

Surprise, shock or disbelief
The information is unexpected, and your reactions can range from mild surprise through to disbelief. You are processing what you've heard, so genuine listening is difficult.

Resistance, denial, denigration
The information doesn't fit your values or expectations or may not make sense to you. Accepting, accommodating the information is near impossible. You might deny or denigrate the information or person. Your focus is myopic, hearing is close to impossible.

Secondary thinking, accommodation
You begin to work with the information, you ruminate on it or discuss with the person. You may be quick or slow. You begin a process of accommodating bits of the information. Hearing is still difficult but you may be open to seeing other viewpoints.

Acceptance, negotiation, change
You begin to accept rather than resist the information and its implications. You are able to listen and negotiate, bargain and adapt your thinking to different possibilities.

REACTIVE LISTENING

Consider the following example, where a combination of autopilot, culture, power and perception shaped someone's listening.

In the early 2000s a UK manufacturer in the Midlands, now closed, faced increasing global competition and was struggling with costs.

A production line operator, Sammi, called her manager to correct faulty components by stopping the line. Under pressure to maintain volume her manager perceived Sammi in a 'perceptual box'. In that box Sammi, like all the floor operatives, was lazy and hunting for ways to down tools. He believed she wasn't capable of or interested in doing a good job.

Driven by perception, beliefs and pressure the boss turned accusatory. He told Sammi the shift was *'foolish for trying it on'* and to *'get back to it'*. Complying, most of the afternoon was spent making faulty goods, until the manager went to the production line and saw what was actually happening.

REACTIVE LISTENING

In the process of receiving unexpected information, where do you think that manager was?

Unexpected information can be very challenging. The more it alters your life the deeper the reaction. Even at a mild level unexpected information can challenge and provoke the reactions.

There are a number of things you might consider when you receive unexpected information:

Notice – note your reaction to the information. What emotions are you experiencing? Fear? Anxiety? Loss? Often labelling them can give you control.

Reflect – what is being challenged in you that is provoking those emotions? Your expectations? Your values? Is the information actually as big a threat as it seems? Is the challenge permanent or temporary in nature? Is it negotiable?

Consider – think about the other person, what their needs are in this moment, what options are appropriate in terms of response.

INTERFERENCES

REACTIVE LISTENING

If you are struggling to process the unexpected information, to move forward: **Breathe!**

Reactions to unexpected information create a negative psychological cycle.

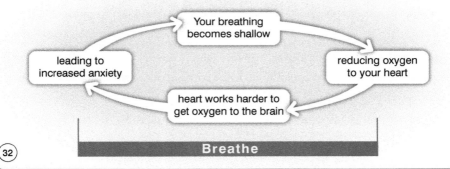

MANAGED LISTENING

The incident described on page 30 didn't close the manufacturer but it was symptomatic of the culture. It also illustrates how power could not restrain itself because it perceived operatives as faulty cogs in the process, cogs not worth listening to. In contrast, consider this example, of an organisation where senior managers were able to manage their reaction to challenging news and genuinely valued their people.

During a major project an employee, Janet, noticed an oversight on the specification sheet supplied by the architects. The firm's suppliers stocked 3-metre workbenches but the architectural drawings for the building specified 4-metre-long workbenches. Janet foresaw increased cost and waste as a consequence of the spec, because for each longer bench they would have to buy two and adapt them. With over 100 benches to be made the additional labour costs alone would eat the profit margin.

The firm's culture valued listening as much as telling and Janet approached the senior managers. They listened because of her credibility and because they were aware of their perceptual 'boxes'. They genuinely believed people had skill, talent and wanted to make a difference.

SUMMARY

This chapter has introduced you to some of the factors that interfere with hearing effectively, including a number of external influences such as the environment, culture and power.

Later chapters will give a more detailed exploration of specific interferences that affect how you interpret what you hear and your consequent response.

Key in the chapter is the notion of you and your own role in your listening. Learn not to take listening for granted but start to question **how** you listen as much as **what** you're listening to.

Listening effectively requires you to step back, think about how you listen and recognise the choice you have to be passive or active in your own listening.

WHAT GOOD LISTENING LOOKS LIKE

WHAT GOOD LISTENING LOOKS LIKE

OVERVIEW

One way of looking at listening is that either you're listening or you're not.

When you're not, or are only half listening, people's radar will pick it up. You might say one thing but a myriad of signs in your tone, body language and responses will show the opposite.

When you listen, people know they've been heard. Your response may challenge what they've said, may differ from what they wanted to hear, but they know their point has been heard and acknowledged. Even with disagreement, good listening makes people feel respected.

This aim of this chapter is to look at that good listening and offer some ways to be more effective. Key to developing your skill is awareness, not just of yourself but of your surroundings. Consciously controlling your listening is important and the chapter presents a useful practical technique, known as levels of listening, to help. In addition, there are principles that can guide your practice in a range of situations from conflict through to influencing.

THE LISTENING STAGES

In a simple form listening moves through a number of stages:

> ***Your hearing alerts you to a noise.***
> Your senses detect something and stimulate you to pay attention.

> ***You listen to the noise.***
> Your senses direct energy to listen and focus on what is being said.

> ***You interpret what you are listening to.***
> Your perception places meaning on what you are listening to.

> ***You respond to what you have listened to.***
> You interpret and translate what you believe was said into a response.

Where are you strong in this process? Can you see where you have work to do?
What would others say were your weak areas?

THE IMPORTANCE OF AWARENESS

Effective listeners monitor how they're listening, or need to listen, in relation to the situation. Awareness of themselves and the surrounding environment enables them to adjust and adapt.

Self-awareness is consciousness of how you're listening, meaning awareness of your physiology, listening habits, energy and focus. For example, is your focus on the other person or on yourself? Are you agitated? Do you need to be calmer, more focused by changing your physiological state?

Environmental awareness is consciousness of external factors such as environment, culture, the person and the interplay between these things. For example, does the physical space need to change because of interfering noise? Is your conversation partner self-conscious, inhibited about speaking in a public space?

Without awareness the habitual autopilot will choose how you listen. Awareness of yourself and the environment is the foundation for choice and control.

WHAT GOOD LISTENING LOOKS LIKE

PRACTISING AWARENESS

Awareness takes practice and like a muscle the more you work it the stronger you get. Next time you're in a conversation at home or at work, mentally step back and observe yourself in various situations.

- Can you notice where your attention is focused? On the other person? On yourself? On the conversation? Are you day dreaming?

- Try the same exercise with people you are familiar and comfortable with, maybe your partner, or family members. Notice how much you are listening to them. Does your listening change depending on context?

- Pay particular attention to the amount of energy you are putting into focusing on the conversation

What should become apparent is that awareness changes and that you choose to turn it up or down.

WHAT GOOD LISTENING LOOKS LIKE

LEVELS OF LISTENING

LOW

A good way to guide your listening and put you, not your autopilot, in control is to use 'levels of listening'. Think of this as a volume control on a radio – you can turn your listening up or down. To do this, engage self- and environmental awareness to judge what level of listening the situation/person needs. You can alter the levels by assessing the energy you're putting into listening and where you are directing your focus. Is it inward to listen to yourself? Or outward to listen to them?

Low level listening – hibernation mode
Energy low
- You hear them but you aren't directing much energy into listening

Focus
- Your focus is inwards, on your own thoughts or nothing in particular
- You're not a zombie but the autopilot is firmly in control

Turn your energy and focus up a notch to shift your listening to **medium.**

WHAT GOOD LISTENING LOOKS LIKE

LEVELS OF LISTENING

MEDIUM

Medium level listening – daily mode

Energy mid-level

- You're listening but the autopilot has the controls

Focus

- Partly outwards to them but mostly directed inwards, listening to yourself
- You're hearing them, you're focused on them and aware of the context
- But autopilot habits still dominate. They shape what you think you hear and your responses

Most of the time people listen from the medium level because it is easy. It is the level where misunderstandings and misinterpretations often occur.

If you're aware and realise the situation demands it you'll know you need to shift your energy and focus up another notch to **high.**

WHAT GOOD LISTENING LOOKS LIKE

LEVELS OF LISTENING

HIGH

High level, high quality listening
Energy high
- Your energy and focus are directed to listening and hearing the person
- You're using energy to maintain awareness of yourself, the person and the context

Focus
- Directed at them, you're aware of your autopilot trying to step in
- You use **all** your faculties to be available to listen to them
- Your **ears** hear the story and how it is told
- Your **eyes** notice changes in body language
- Your **intuition** and **knowledge** listen for what's between the lines
- You're aware that your autopilot/habits are trying to interfere but you can manage them

At this level listening is tiring but is powerful and enabling.

At this level you are 'psychologically available' to hear your conversation partner.

WHAT GOOD LISTENING LOOKS LIKE

BEING PSYCHOLOGICALLY AVAILABLE

When someone isn't psychologically available to listen effectively it is apparent. The slight glaze across the eyes tells you they're not there or their glances across your shoulder tell you they want to be elsewhere.

Your psychological availability affects the quality of your listening and, critically, the quality of connection you form.

Being psychologically available to be at the highest level of listening means:

- Being mentally 'free' to listen. You are not distracted or half-focused on the person, and you have enough time

- Maintaining empathy for whoever you are listening to

- Viewing them as a human being, not an object, with needs as valid as yours

- Being genuine and responsive to what you hear

WHAT GOOD LISTENING LOOKS LIKE

BECOMING PSYCHOLOGICALLY AVAILABLE

Making yourself psychologically available is something you can perfect with practice.

Mindfulness can help in that regard. If you're aware of the need to be psychologically available, turn your attention to yourself and your physiology and do a quick mental scan of Breath, Body, Location and Breathing (BBLB).

> **B**reath – what is your breathing like? Fast, slow, normal?
>
> **B**ody – what is the state of your body? Are you agitated, relaxed, tense?
>
> **L**ocation – where in your body do those feelings reside, eg, stomach, legs, chest?
>
> **B**reathing – using slow, deep breathing, focusing on your breath and releasing any of the tensions, can alter your state and help you become available. When you're available you are focused on the present, not on what has happened nor what you think should happen but on **what is happening now.**

Continue to practise and you will get better at noticing and altering your state.

PURPOSEFUL LISTENING PRINCIPLES

Many situations can cause you to be 'unavailable' and to drop your level of listening: conflict, for example, or receiving challenging information, or pressure. The following principles underpin the level of listening and help you to maintain focus. They're not easy, in fact they are challenging to apply, but they're beneficial.

- **Genuine openness** – means reacting honestly to what you hear. It doesn't mean being passive or unconditionally accepting of everything you hear; to do so would damage your credibility. Genuine openness enables you to see people with human needs rather than objects whilst maintaining respect and assertiveness. A colleague calls it 'hard head, warm heart'

- **Empathy** – helps maintain a warm heart and strengthens connections. Even if you must challenge what has been said, empathy maintains your perception of your conversation partner as a human being. This is because to empathise you need to try to understand how someone feels by imagining what it's like in their position

WHAT GOOD LISTENING LOOKS LIKE

PURPOSEFUL LISTENING PRINCIPLES

Three further principles are:

- **Positive regard** – this means maintaining respect and admiration for the person and being willing to support them, no matter the size of difference between your perspectives or gap in power

- **Curiosity** – helps you to overcome prejudice and the risk of viewing someone through a perceptual box, because curiosity drives you to explore. Curiosity is a visible demonstration of interest and desire to know more about the person as an individual not an object

- **Non-judgemental listening** – there may be some situations where suspending judgement will benefit all parties. Listening non-judgementally is challenging to do and takes practice, but done well it strengthens the quality of connection

THE PROCESS & CONTENT OF STORIES

Another useful skill is discerning the difference between content and process and why that difference is important when listening. Simply put:

Content is the story being told, the details of who did what, the problems to overcome, the heroes, villains and victims, etc.

Process is how the story is told, the emotions invested in the narrative, inflections on words, pauses, gestures, how the story is structured, etc.

BE WARY OF THE LURE OF DETAIL

Often, the content of someone else's story leads you to think about your own experiences. The content and detail of what they are saying draws you in; you relate to and make sense of their story through your personal experience. When that occurs, your focus moves to your own thoughts and you stop listening. For example:

- You become immersed in the detail and lose track of what is important

- Personal memories are triggered, your focus shifts to hearing your own stories and you lose track of the other person

- If the story connects with deeply held values, memories or expectations, you might lose track of the entire conversation

When you are listening to a story, pay attention to how the person relates to the content. You can feed back observations and highlight things they may not have been aware of. For example, if the content makes them proud: *'It sounds like you were pleased with how you handled that client's situation'*.

WHAT GOOD LISTENING LOOKS LIKE

LISTEN TO HOW A STORY IS TOLD

How a story is told, the process, is just as valuable to notice as the details. Process might be inflections, sighs and gestures, all of which are visible demonstrations of someone's internal state.

Noticing how someone is telling their story, their gestures, pace, changes in tone will show you what's important or pressing on their mind.

Again, notice and feed back your observations, *'I noticed when you mentioned the funding that your tone changed, went lower, and your shoulders slumped'*. You can help them gain awareness and further insight about themselves and what has most meaning in the context.

WHAT GOOD LISTENING LOOKS LIKE

PULLING EVERYTHING TOGETHER

The level of listening model is most effective when you're psychologically available and guided by the principles of genuine openness, empathy, and so on. Each level will have a different effect. Take this example:

An energetic and committed junior manager, Danny, had begun an informal mentoring relationship with a senior manager. Danny found interpreting financial spreadsheets a challenge and wanted to address his issue. Feeling secure he told the senior manager/mentor, Marie, towards the end of their next informal meeting. Marie had an impending meeting at another site.

What was said:

> *'I'm keen to develop in my role, I like the challenge and find it interesting but I find .....uhm ...... financial spreadsheets hard work and, if I'm ....uhm....... honest, don't particularly understand how to .... uhm... interpret them. It hasn't been part of my work before.'*

LEVELS OF LISTENING IN PRACTICE

LOW LEVEL LISTENING

 At low level listening the autopilot is well and truly in control and Marie might be thinking:

'Financial spreadsheets are a pain, yes I get that. But thinking about pain, I've got that meeting in 10 minutes on the other side of the building and still need to get my folder. Hmm, I haven't really prepared for it, but I don't have to do much in the meeting so it should be okay. How long do I need to be here – shouldn't Danny talk to finance about this?'

So the autopilot response might be:

'Talk to finance about it, I'm sure they've got something to sort you out. I've just realised I have a meeting to get to; tell me how you get on next week.'

How 'available' is Marie? What principles can you see? How might Danny react to that response, in the first instance? Later? Could there be a longer-term effect?

WHAT GOOD LISTENING LOOKS LIKE

LEVELS OF LISTENING IN PRACTICE

MEDIUM LEVEL LISTENING

At **medium** level the autopilot still has the controls but there is recognition of some of the issues the person faces. Marie might be thinking:

'It's great hearing Danny's enthusiasm, we need energetic people. I don't understand the problem with financial spreadsheets – we all need to know them and they are pretty straightforward. I need to be at that meeting at the other site. I know what he can do, just sort it out with his line manager. I did that, it worked for me.'

The spoken response, driven by her experience and comfort with the subject, might be:

'What you ought to do is see your line manager. I did that when I was in your role. Once you get used to spreadsheets they're easy, anyone can do them. You'll be fine.'

How 'available' is Marie in this instance? To what extent do you think this response would help Danny? What level of motivation do you think he'd have for moving the issue forward?

WHAT GOOD LISTENING LOOKS LIKE

LEVELS OF LISTENING IN PRACTICE

HIGH LEVEL LISTENING

Perhaps something in Danny's tone, or the way he shifted and looked down, alerted Marie to dial up her listening and availability. Perhaps she thought:

> *'I know Danny is ambitious and sets high expectations for himself. He was hesitant and looked down when he said he didn't particularly understand; perhaps he feels vulnerable? I'm okay interpreting financial spreadsheets but I notice his concern. That is quite a risk opening up about his lack of confidence, not easy to do, particularly with a senior manager. That takes courage. I wonder what's happening with his line manager. It seems odd that three months into the role there isn't a development plan.'*

High level listening is where genuine openness, empathy, positive regard, curiosity and non-judgemental listening come into play.

WHAT GOOD LISTENING LOOKS LIKE

LEVELS OF LISTENING IN PRACTICE

HIGH LEVEL LISTENING

 Marie's response to what she heard and noticed would now sound like this:

> *'Thanks for being open about interpreting financial spreadsheets. I can see you're worried and that you want to be thorough; we appreciate your high standards. You're right about financial spreadsheets, interpreting them is an important part of the role, and it is not uncommon for people to get white noise when they look at them. It's important we build your skills and confidence. What discussions have you had with your line manager about this?'*

Listening seems a simple skill but it is not easy to tune your radar, notice what is happening and respond to what you see and hear. Emotional intelligence is needed to suddenly be available, suspend judgement, and maintain empathy. To change in the moment takes practice and belief in the benefit that effective, high level listening offers.

In the actual situation the manager's response had been, *'I'm surprised, you ought to know those, do we need to go back to basics with you?'* What do you suppose the outcomes were?

BUILD YOUR SKILLS

Great listening takes effort and practice. The more you practise the easier and more familiar it becomes. Spend some time practising being available, working on the principles and changing the level you are listening at. Try these exercises:

- In the middle of conversations consciously check where your focus and energy are; check how 'available' you think you are to your conversation partners

- Try suspending judgement when listening – don't focus on right or wrong, focus on how the other person relates to the story and what was meaningful to him or her

- When you're in a familiar setting with family or friends, try 'dialling up' your listening and notice what is different

- Over a series of encounters increase your level of listening with someone you normally find hard to listen to and notice if anything changes between you over the period. Try using positive regard for them (page 46) and see if you notice a difference

- Spend time observing people you know. See if you can determine how available they make themselves and the level of their listening

GOOD LISTENING IN SUMMARY

This chapter has covered a range of aspects relating to good listening, from practical tools such as the levels of listening through to underlying principles and psychological availability. This is because effective listening requires more than simple behavioural techniques.

Effective listening means putting yourself aside to focus on the other person. Effective listening is not passive or weak. Good listening is powerful and assertive because you can hear with greater clarity what is important to someone and consequently what they need and will respond to.

To do so your ego and autopilot need to be out of the equation.

BLOCKS TO ACCURATE INTERPRETATION

BLOCKS TO ACCURATE INTERPRETATION

INTRODUCTION

Remember the second scenario in the introduction? The manager, a medium level listener, focused more on her own concerns than on those of the speaker.

Inside and outside work that scenario is common because most people, you and me included, rely on habitual, medium level listening and responding. The habits you've built from a young age are part and parcel of who you are. Their familiarity makes you blind to them, which is why they're very difficult to change.

Those medium level listening habits are called 'blocks to listening' and interfere with what you hear. They are so familiar that you're barely conscious of how they affect your interpretation of what people say and mean.

BLOCKS TO ACCURATE INTERPRETATION

INTRODUCTION

The blocks shape your response because through them you convert what was actually said into what you think and believe was said. There are 12: each will be covered in this chapter with guidance on how to recognise them and what you can do to manage them. The blocks are:

1. Advising
2. Being right/being competitive
3. Comparing
4. Derailing

5. Faking attention
6. Fight or flight
7. Filtering
8. Identifying

9. Judging
10. Placating
11. Rehearsing
12. Sparring

Their impact varies. Some are relatively minor, perhaps just signalling that you're a poor listener. Others, if habitual, can make you someone people might avoid. Once aware of the blocks try observing other people and see if you can spot any blocks in action. Observe yourself too. If willing, ask for feedback to see if you have habitual ones.

Become aware of your habitual blocks and you'll be able to manage them instead of them managing you.

BLOCKS TO ACCURATE INTERPRETATION

1 ADVISING

Advising is a very common block to listening because people are born problem-solvers. On hearing someone tell a problem most people switch to solution mode. Sometimes solution mode is appropriate, but often it can disempower people.

You'll know you've moved to advising when you're impatient to tell them what they should do, or what you'd do in their place. Your attention is on your solutions, on convincing them to agree; you've stopped hearing them and what they're trying to say.

You might move the issue forward in the short term and build a reputation as the go to person. You can, however, dampen enthusiasm, disempower problem-solving and curb confidence. Habitually 'advising' indicates you trust your judgement more than others', that you struggle to be flexible or able to let go or to make yourself available for developing others.

Keep doing it and you may find you're the permanent problem-solver, again, and again, and again.

BLOCKS TO ACCURATE INTERPRETATION

1 ADVISING – WHAT TO DO

Notice if you're impatient to provide a solution. If you are, bite your tongue! Swallow your desire to push the solution on them! Give them space to think.

Manage your physiological reaction, if the compulsion feels strong. For example, use slow, deep breathing to keep your focus on them and pace yourself.

Try using questions instead of solutions, questions guided by curiosity and positive regard to help both of you explore their perspective, for example, *'What is the key problem you want to solve?'*; *'What would be a good outcome, for you, for others?'*; *'What have you done in other situations?'*

If you really, really can't hold back, then parcel your suggestions as an offer: *'I have some ideas I'll share. If you think they'll work we can explore them but if not we'll move on'*. If your listening has shifted to the high level you'll pick up whether your idea has traction.

2 BEING RIGHT/BEING COMPETITIVE

Being right/being competitive means going to any length to avoid being wrong. You do not listen to criticism, do not like being corrected, and won't accept suggestions for change. You've blocked your flexibility to listen and adapt because your attention is on self-protection.

In the short term, you've the satisfaction of being right and winning. Longer term, people might find you tiresome. You will seem insecure, unreceptive to new ideas and learning. You're liable to continue making mistakes if your listening prevents you from hearing and acknowledging feedback.

Develop a reputation for being right/being competitive and people are likely to go elsewhere for discussion and debate when dealing with complex decisions.

BLOCKS TO ACCURATE INTERPRETATION

2 BEING RIGHT/BEING COMPETITIVE – WHAT TO DO

If your need to be right/be competitive is strong then switching your awareness on can be a challenge. There are two areas to consider if you want to improve in this area: what you can do during a conversation and what you can do between conversations.

During a conversation – it's important that your awareness is engaged, and that you shift your focus to the other person. Use empathy to listen, imagining how the situation appears from their perspective. Use curiosity to find what is important to them or the main point they are trying to convey.

Between conversations – observe yourself, to see if there are particular situations or people that trigger this block. Notice what physiological symptoms arise when this block is engaged, symptoms such as tension, agitation, etc. Doing so can help you spot early warning signs. You can learn to manage reactions before they become responses.

BLOCKS TO ACCURATE INTERPRETATION

 **COMPARING**

Comparing is when, while engaged in conversation, you're trying to work out which of you is smarter, more experienced, has higher status, etc. It is human nature to compare yourself with others – it gives you a benchmark for yourself and the process of comparing can be a catalyst to develop yourself further.

Your listening is blocked, however, when comparing becomes a fixation. Your attention is driven by your insecurities and your focus is on the comparisons you are making. Rather than interaction with the topic under discussion, your conversation partner will be faced with someone presenting themselves as higher or lower status.

They may hear, *'Oh yes when I did ....'* or *'I have done that too except what I did was....'* Or, alternatively, *'You're so much better at those things than me; I wish I was as good.'* Instead of discussion you have a game of top trumps or false humility. The conversation ends up being side-tracked.

3 COMPARING – WHAT TO DO

Use your awareness to check your attitude and feelings towards the person. Be honest and ask yourself hard questions. Is the comparison being driven by envy of them? Are they a threat? What do they have that you want? Is it a healthy rivalry or is the process of comparing interfering with your ability to hear them?

During a conversation – focus your attention on their strengths. Endeavour to notice their unique qualities and strengths and feed them back into the conversation: *'I notice you're good at seeing solutions to problems in the department.' 'It's helpful the way you respond quickly and on your own initiative to the client'.* Doing so acknowledges you've seen and appreciate them.

Between conversations – acknowledge that everyone brings something different to the mix. Clarify your strengths instead of feeling threatened by others. Work to become clear, skilled and confident in how you use your strengths and the value you add.

BLOCKS TO ACCURATE INTERPRETATION

4 DERAILING

Derailing is when you change the subject suddenly. You might do this dramatically or subtly, with humour a common tactic. Your motives could be boredom, unfamiliarity with the subject, discomfort with the topic or person or discomfort with the pace because you're two steps ahead.

Your listening is blocked because your attention is directed towards escaping or moving the subject and person on. They may find themselves wrong-footed or feel insecure because their flow of thinking has been disrupted. They may, if they've come to discuss something sensitive, feel they've misjudged the level of intimacy or support you offer them.

Derailing gives you temporary relief from discomfort. However, the other person will know your attention has been elsewhere. People may feel unsettled by you and withhold information in future. They will keep conversations at a superficial level and for important discussions seek someone they feel respected by and secure with.

BLOCKS TO ACCURATE INTERPRETATION

4 DERAILING – WHAT TO DO

Pay attention to see how often you derail. Even minor levels are worth noting – a quip to lighten the mood may seem harmless but you can throw someone off their train of thought. Do it frequently and it may cause them to think you don't respect them. Try to notice any patterns: when, where and with whom. Ask yourself the reasons why you derail.

Notice what happens when you change topic suddenly. What tactics do you use? Humour? Total change of subject? What is the effect on the other person? Watch their reaction – subtle facial clues might indicate an inner frustration. Do they withdraw from the conversation?

Learn to hold the desire to derail. If you begin to feel agitated maintain your focus on the other person but shift position, stand, move about to regain control. Chapter 4, Responding, has a range of listening strategies you may find of help in this area.

BLOCKS TO ACCURATE INTERPRETATION

5 FAKING ATTENTION

Faking attention is when you half listen. You may be bored, have low energy, or find the subject triggering personal memories. You dial down to low level listening, daydreaming or with your attention on nothing in particular. You've mentally 'checked out' and aren't psychologically available to listen.

Everyone is human and fakes attention at some time or another. If a considered response is required, however, or you're asked about a specific aspect of the discussion, your lack of presence may become apparent to all. Another consequence of faking attention is that you will miss the true point of what someone is trying to say.

5 FAKING ATTENTION – WHAT TO DO

If you're aware of frequently faking attention, assess the cause. Is it tiredness? Diary management? Low blood sugar levels? A toilet break needed?

Kate, a senior manager, was regularly involved in meetings where listening was crucial because deeply emotive subjects were discussed, but became aware that diary commitments affected her ability to listen.

Her meetings were frequently back to back. She had little time to consolidate one before moving to the next, and little time to look after herself because lunch was always on the run. Kate reviewed her commitments, scheduling space either side of important meetings to allow time to prepare. Her listening effectiveness increased because a simple thing like eating well maintained her blood sugar levels, and going to the toilet meant she could focus on the person rather than her physical discomfort.

Another cause of faking attention can be lack of respect. If you find that you are regularly faking attention with the same person be honest with yourself about your respect for them. Try changing your frame of reference and noticing their qualities and strengths.

BLOCKS TO ACCURATE INTERPRETATION

6 FIGHT OR FLIGHT

One phenomenon that can easily catch you unawares and prevent you from listening is when you are threatened, challenged. Your brain isn't too good at distinguishing between actual threat and implied threat. A social challenge to deeply held aspects of yourself, for example your values, identity or credibility, whilst not physically harmful, is nonetheless perceived as threatening.

In mediation it is called being 'hooked'. Your higher-level thinking reduces as the primal brain takes over, adrenaline and strong emotions pushing you to **fight or flight**. You lose perspective, you don't listen, you close down possibilities and, critically, you disempower yourself, resorting to childish survival strategies.

6 FIGHT OR FLIGHT – WHAT TO DO

When the fight or flight impulse kicks in, you're not hearing anyone or anything; you're fighting to protect something deep inside you.

If you sense that you're hooked, **stop, pause, breathe** and **focus** on the other person. If need be, give yourself space, asking to pause proceedings whilst you process what you have heard. If you've stopped hearing, you've lost control.

BLOCKS TO ACCURATE INTERPRETATION

7 FILTERING

Filtering is when you listen for, or hear, some things and not others. In other words, you hear what you want to hear. Filtering helps reduce the volume of things to concentrate on. However it also blocks your ability to hear and work creatively. For example:

A café manager asked a customer if she had enjoyed her lunch. All the techniques of good listening were on show: good eye contact, inviting smile, attentive body language. After a pause the woman responded politely and factually with, 'The food was nice though the portion sizes didn't match the description'. It wasn't aggressive or accusatory and seemed a useful piece of feedback.

The conversation immediately became adversarial. The manager focused on one part of the message, the bit perceived as negative, and consequently filtered out the praise. For whatever reason (an inability to accept criticism, however constructive, perhaps), the manager did not hear or respond to the kindly attempt to provide useful feedback and made it clear that he thought the customer was ill-informed.

From the customer's evident discomfort, her relationship with the café was irrevocably changed.

7 FILTERING – WHAT TO DO

As a consequence, the café manager missed both the overall message and the opportunity to address a concern and strengthen a future relationship. Filtering reduces your ability to hear the range and context of what is being conveyed. Missed are opportunities to gain insight, work with generative feedback and seek collaborative solutions.

Some of the blocks, eg derailing or advising, are obvious when you become aware of them. Others such as filtering are subtler and need higher degrees of self-observation and honesty.

During a conversation pay close attention to yourself. Are you hearing the whole message or noticing select items? Do particular things capture your attention? For example, some people hear feelings in preference to logic. Your goals or expectations might direct you to focus on specific aspects but neglect others.

Chapter 4, Responding, has a tool called summarising. To summarise effectively you need to listen at a high level to hear the key themes. You'll know how well you've heard the whole message by the indirect verbal or physical feedback from the other person, for example nods of agreement, changes in tone, etc.

BLOCKS TO ACCURATE INTERPRETATION

8 IDENTIFYING

Identifying is when you compare what you're hearing against your own experience. Doing so helps make sense of what is being said and creates common ground. You can relate to the person and their story: *'I've had similar happen to me....'*

Your ability to hear is blocked when your recollections dominate and, like **advising**, you can't wait to put your story front and centre of the conversation. You take the conversation from them to you. Your eagerness to share your story (whatever the motive) prevents the person from conveying the point or connection they're trying to make.

Many managers forget that the weight of their role, their power, causes people to defer to them. Conversation partners may appear to be listening to your wisdom but inside they may be irritated that the conversation has become about you. Habitual identifying will win you a reputation of only being interested in yourself.

BLOCKS TO ACCURATE INTERPRETATION

8 IDENTIFYING – WHAT TO DO

Notice who has the majority of airtime, you or them. If you suspect it is you, hit pause, turn off the autopilot and step back from your need to tell your story. Increase the level of listening to hear the full story, not just the bits that strike a chord with you.

An easy strategy is silence. Create space to listen for what is meaningful to them. Feed back what you hear and notice, eg: *'That sounded a significant event for you?'; 'I can see from the way you're talking how important it was'; 'I noticed a change in your tone and pace as you explained your observations – you seemed more urgent. Is that correct?'*

Questions underpinned by curiosity and positive regard demonstrate your interest. By all means share your experiences, that is part of the flow of conversations, but avoid taking it off on your tangent.

BLOCKS TO ACCURATE INTERPRETATION

 **JUDGING**

Judging is when you hold preformed conclusions about the other person. Everybody does it as it helps form first impressions and categorise inner and outer circles of trusted people. Judging has a powerful influence on what you hear because once you've formed a judgement about someone you'll stick to it.

An easy way to think of judging is through a cognitive bias called *the horns and halo effect*. In simple terms, you judge people as positive (halo) or negative (horns). You look and listen for evidence to confirm your judgement (who wants to be wrong, eh?). If they are 'halo' you regard everything they do and say in a positive light. If they make a mistake you'll find allowances for it. 'Horns' is the opposite, where your view is always negative.

Your ability to listen objectively, notice strengths, weaknesses and potential is blocked because everything you hear, similar to the Midlands production manager on page 30, is processed through your judgement.

9 JUDGING – WHAT TO DO

Like Josh with the 'worst employee in the world' (page 27), once you have formed a judgement you rarely change it. Ask yourself whether you've labelled someone. If so, undermine your judgements by asking yourself whether there might be other explanations for their behaviour. Are you in some way contributing to their behaviour or are you looking at them through a cognitive bias?

A challenging but beneficial skill is the ability to suspend judgement. Your focus shifts to hearing them rather than confirming your bias. Use empathy and positive regard to guide your responses, for example, *'I have some idea how that situation may have been a challenge for you'*. Try the summarising technique in Chapter 4, Responding.

He's lying

10 PLACATING

Placating is when you try to stop someone feeling angry or offended by being nice to them. In some situations placating may well be required to defuse or redirect emotions.

However, if placating is habitual your ability to listen and help solve problems is hampered. Your attention is more on protecting yourself from strong emotions than hearing the issues people are discussing. Your psychological availability to help the person move forward is limited, and people may get the impression that venting or catharsis is not allowed.

Habitual placating doesn't address issues, allowing them to fester and become more entrenched. People may feel patronised and not heard, which can escalate disputes.

10 PLACATING – WHAT TO DO

Firstly, notice if you are trying to avoid either the person or something in the conversation. Use mindfulness, (see page 44 for BBLB: Breath Body Location Breathing), to notice and manage sensations before the sensations manage you. Secondly, when anxiety arises learn to recognise and manage it.

For example, a mediator I worked with was aware that anxiety, triggered by strong client emotions, manifested as tension in his chest and shallow breathing, leading to anxiety and subjectivity. His approach was to slow his breathing down and imagine the tension as a ball he could mentally shift to the base of his stomach. These steps helped him retain physiological, mental and emotional control and continue to listen well.

Clarify what causes you to placate. Often, once identified and labelled, the discomfort eases. Observe yourself, learn how and where anxiety manifests. Learn to 'sit' with it, try psychological techniques to shift anxiety and retain control. You can even turn the discomfort into a useful question: *'I'm feeling unsure about this, is that similar for you?'*

11 REHEARSING

Rehearsing is when you're preparing your response whilst the other person is speaking. Everyone rehearses because it is natural to anticipate what someone is saying. The block on your listening occurs when, at some point in the discussion, you form a conclusion or judgement and stop hearing anything further. Everything they say from that point onwards delays **you** from getting your point across.

The classic sign that you've been rehearsing is when people hear you say *'Yes ..... but'* or *'That sounds great ..... but'* or *'I hear what you're saying ..... but'*. These phrases show you're listening at mid-level – you've stopped listening to them in order to listen to yourself.

Your ability to hear new ideas, insights, creative opportunities or concepts that challenge you is reduced because your mind closed once your conclusion formed.

BLOCKS TO ACCURATE INTERPRETATION

11 REHEARSING – WHAT TO DO

Firstly, pay attention to your 'self-talk', the inner voice rattling inside your head. As your colleague is speaking thoughts may arise: *'That won't work because ...'* or *'She knows I've done a huge amount so how can she say that? I'll just have to tell her about ......'.* Notice your physiology: is the urge to rebut strong? Who's getting the attention, your inner voice or them?

Push the inner voice to the back of your mind along with the rehearsals and rebuttals. Use mindfulness to focus and notice what is happening at that point in time.

A useful structure for responding is YOU, ME, AGREE

> **YOU** – allow them time to speak, listen and explore key points.

> **ME** – you then outline your points.

> **AGREE** – summarise points of agreement, highlight where there is no agreement and explore to problem-solve.

12 SPARRING

Sparring is when you argue or debate in order to 'win' or dominate the conversation. It is an extension of **being right/competitive.** You appear to argue for argument's sake rather than to gain new insight or reach common understanding. Sparring is not to be confused with being assertive. Assertiveness requires you to acknowledge and respect people's right to different viewpoints.

If you're sparring, your ability to engage others and hear different points of view is reduced because you are not hearing what is meaningful to them. Your attention is on continually shifting the ground, finding points of disagreement rather than connection.

You may think you are being strong and assertive but spar habitually and people will find you frustrating and tiresome because you're never willing to compromise or concede a point.

(82) People will feel you don't listen to them.

BLOCKS TO ACCURATE INTERPRETATION

 SPARRING – WHAT TO DO

If sparring is deeply ingrained in your approach it can be hard to identify. Honest self-reflection and courage to seek feedback from others may be needed. Ask yourself if it's important that your views/opinions are accepted as being 'right', no matter the importance of the subject or relationship.

If you notice you frequently spar, hold your tongue. Try building a firewall between stimuli and response by counting to three before responding. Try responding with observations rather than counterarguments. Pay attention to their process, feed back what you notice about how they tell the story, inflections, important points, etc. Doing so will demonstrate you are paying attention to them and potentially deepen their thinking about themselves.

It might be useful to reflect longer term on the reputation you want: an adversarial bore or someone who listens and illuminates.

BLOCKS TO ACCURATE INTERPRETATION

SUMMARY

The blocks on your listening and interpretation are difficult areas to identify because they are so ingrained and habitual. They are also, some more than others, very, very frustrating to be on the receiving end of. Who wants to be in a conversation with someone so competitive that they always have to be right?

A good place to start understanding and recognising your blocks is to practise the levels of listening (page 40) and underlying principles. The more you practise the more you'll notice the blocks at work and become familiar with your self-talk.

Another way to detect them is though using mindfulness techniques, like the ones on pages 44 and also 31. They can help you become more attuned to bodily sensations, such as tension and agitation, which are early warning signals. The signals are faint because your focus is elsewhere but they are there and you will find them very useful as you learn to manage yourself.

Manage yourself and you begin to manage the blocks.

RESPONDING

INTRODUCTION

Hmmm

The way you respond tells someone not only how well you've heard them but also how you relate to and regard them. Your responses don't have to be big, demonstrative or overly controlling. You can use small gestures, an incline of the head, or noises of encouragement, or observations that show you're available to hear. Fitting responses nudge conversations forward, nudge speakers to go further.

This chapter presents a range of ways of responding. Some are structures to help you listen with purpose and demonstrate you are hearing what is important. Some are skills and ways of 'being' such as silence, while others require awareness of whether to railroad a conversation for control or keep it open for possibilities.

The aim of the chapter is to further broaden your choice in how you listen and respond.

QUESTIONS

Questions are the bread and butter of responding. There are many types of question and many ways to structure them but the simplest place to start is to differentiate between open and closed questions. Part of the skill with questions is knowing when to use which type.

Open questions are expansive and give people space to respond. Open questions do not limit someone to 'yes' or 'no'. They are useful because they stimulate people to think through their responses and can encourage reflection, learning and insight.

Open questions are powerful tools for developing people's thinking, problem-solving skills and confidence. Used with skill, they can be transformational.

For example, the question *'Were you pleased the project meeting was successful?'* has a yes/no response and allows little room for elaboration. The question is transactional. The open question *'What do you think were the reasons for the success of the project meeting?'* is expansive and gives permission to reflect and clarify insights.

OPEN QUESTIONS

Open questions typically use the prefixes:

- How – *'How did the relationship with the new customer begin?'*
- What – *'What did you do about the late delivery of the project plan?'*
- When – *'When did it become apparent that you needed to step into the role?'*
- Who – *'Who else do you need to have involved in order to support you and the team?'*

One prefix to be careful with is *'Why'*. It is habitual and reactive to ask 'why' but the word can appear accusatory and is often used when blame is being handed out. It can also feel parental. In the face of 'why' people can move to defend themselves or feel embarrassed that they don't know the answer.

Next time 'why' is on the tip of your tongue reach for an alternative. Instead of *'Why did you let that happen?'* ask *'What do you think were the reasons for it happening?'* See what response you get.

CLOSED QUESTIONS

Closed questions seek a clear answer. Typically, they require a 'yes' or 'no' response. The focus, generally, of closed questions is to check if things have happened or are going to happen. For example:

> 'Did you submit the latest project plan drafts?'

> 'Have you passed the new operating procedures to the rest of the shift?'

Closed questions are useful when people have clarified their thinking following open questions, or when time is tight and you need a short sharp yes/no answer.

LEADING QUESTIONS

Asking good questions takes skill. It is only too easy to respond using a leading question presented in the guise of an open question, eg:

'Do you think you should ......?'

'Wouldn't you think it better to....?'

The message your conversation partner will hear is, *'I'm going through the motions of asking and listening to you but the truth is I trust my knowledge and experience more than yours'.*

Far better to declare your intention than to ask a leading question. For example, *'Personally I think the following should happen but you also have a role in this so it would be good to hear your ideas'.* Genuine openness with positive regard is more authentic, honest and trustworthy than manipulative leading questions.

SILENCE

Many people find silence the most challenging response to master. One reason is that you can feel a compulsion to respond as soon as someone has finished talking. Another is that some people feel their identity and credibility rest on 'having the answer'.

Yet silence, your ability not to respond immediately, can be a powerful demonstration of listening. Silence provides reflective space. People frequently go on to clarify what they have just said because how something sounds, and its logic, differ when spoken aloud.

Silence can be a visible demonstration of respect for the person and what they have just said. You can also buy time with silence if you're not clear about their response – hold your nerve and they will add more detail.

Practise silence by counting to five before responding. Silence can be filled with gestures, nods, smiles, encouragement to go on. It is easy to do and hard to master.

SUMMARISING

Summarising is feeding back in a concise manner the key themes. It is powerful for a number of reasons:

- To summarise effectively **you have to listen**. Listen at a low/medium level and you'll merely put your spin on what you've heard, revealing how self-interested you are

- Summarising is a clear sign of positive regard because they can see you've been listening

- It helps sort the 'wheat from the chaff' because it makes you discern and feed back what is important, which can be helpful to both of you

Great listening is when you summarise key points from both content and process. For example: *'From what you've just said it seems the key things are that you have limited authority yet you have received a grant of over £2 million. When you mentioned the amount of money you sounded like a heavy weight was on you because your tone of voice and pace of speaking changed'*.

RESPONDING

CLARIFYING

Clarifying is a pause button that helps you check what you've heard.

Stories are often non-linear. As memories are refreshed and new insights and connections between events occur people loop back and adjust their story.

Stories also have omissions. Tellers might assume you're familiar with the context or details or may forget to include elements that connect different parts of the story. Connecting the threads can be hard work and sometimes the story moves on whilst you're still trying to fathom out earlier details.

CLARIFYING

Clarifying is simple. You interrupt to pause the story and test what is important to the teller. For example:

'I need to check I've heard things accurately. You appear to be saying that you met Jamal from the supply company last week and you agreed a price and delivery schedule. But since you handed the contract finalisation to admin support it hasn't moved forward. They are saying nothing was sent to them?'

Clarifying displays positive regard and curiosity because you're demonstrating you're following the story. If you're accurate they'll concur, if not they'll clarify the key points and you'll both be on the same page.

FOCUSING

Focusing can be used when the point or purpose of the conversation isn't clear. Perhaps your conversation partner has gone off at a tangent, perhaps they are offloading. For example, they may come to you about one thing: *'the problem with the budgeting system is the authorisation process'* and without pause shift to another topic: *'and that reminds me of something transport did the other week regarding days in lieu ....'*

Perhaps they've globalised by escalating an issue to a higher level. In other words they feel they cannot take action on a local issue because the overall cause is beyond their control. For example:

'I've struggled to get my planning done because of staff shortages. I need temporary staff. But to get approval I need to go to my manager and she's hard to get hold of because she is always at strategy meetings, so I never know the forecast. Senior management don't realise the pressure we're under and make policies that hamper us.'

Globalising disempowers people – they believe it is beyond them to solve the issue because it is all 'too big'.

(95)

FOCUSING

Your time is valuable and focusing with a 'hard head and warm heart' can be helpful for managing time whilst maintaining empathy and positive regard. There are a number of techniques you can use to help someone focus:

- Bring the issue back to their sphere of influence – *'How does this issue affect you?'*

- Challenge them to clarify – *'There is a lot of detail but it is not clear what your key issue is'*

- Raise awareness of your time and outcome – *'The issue sounds significant but beyond the time I have now. If we meet again in an hour could you be clear what you want from me?'*

- Direct challenge – *'What is the bottom line for you in this?'* or *'What is your contribution to the problem?'*

RESPONDING

FEN

FEN is a summarising technique to help you listen and respond. FEN is useful because it can help you read between the lines of what someone is saying.

To use FEN you need to listen at the highest level, looking out for:

F acts – what are the facts of the story?

E motions – what emotions are present and how are they being expressed?

N eeds – what needs are being expressed? Generally, needs will not be expressed clearly but through the emotions.

On the next page we look at an example of a mediation case between two neighbours that involved music and noise in the late evening. The person who'd raised the complaint was elderly, agitated, frustrated and angry.

RESPONDING

FEN

'There are nights when he comes in and is really noisy; he doesn't have any consideration. The walls are thin and I can hear him come up the stairs, then the music goes on. It is loud and keeps my wife and me awake for ages. It is not fair, he is a big man and always seems annoyed in the mornings when I'm up and see him. I don't like having to deal with this in my own home.'

The **Facts** were tiredness, noise, timing, shared space and thin walls and that he hadn't actually spoken to the neighbour. **Emotions** were frustration with not knowing what to do, resentment and fear about the neighbour because of his looks. The **Needs**, not directly expressed, were to feel safe in his own house and continue being a protector to his wife.

Using FEN as a listening and summarising tool helped clarify the core issues and identify ways forward. The neighbour, as it turned out, worked shifts, was tired in the mornings and didn't realise the volume was loud.

TESTING ASSUMPTIONS & PERMISSIONS

You make assumptions when you listen to others; everyone does. Assumptions are important because they help you fill in the gaps in a story or enable you to attribute deeper meaning. For example you might assume the reason for a particular action.

It is critical to recognise when you make assumptions, otherwise they can morph into facts. When you respond, test any assumption you've made: *'I have assumed that …'*.

A powerful method to check and test your assumptions, indeed a powerful tool in any hierarchical relationship, is the use of permission. Permissions are particularly helpful when you are speaking from a position of authority. They work on the basis that you give permission to be corrected.

When summarising, clarifying or testing assumptions you can start by saying, *'Let me know if I don't give an accurate reflection …'* or *'I am going to offer a suggestion. If it works, that's great. If not just say so and we'll drop it'* or *'I'm assuming you wanted to do X, let me know if that isn't correct'*.

Permissions don't mean you lose power or control.

CHALLENGING

How do you respond when you hear something that is incorrect, or doesn't fit your understanding or the organisation's needs? You may feel you need to 'challenge what was said'. Yet 'challenge' is a loaded word. It can turn a response into a confrontation, implying that something important is at stake.

If you want to defuse and problem-solve rather than escalate and confront there are other ways of framing a challenge. For example, *'I want to gain some clarity'*, or *'understand what was said'*.

The most honest response is to clarify what has challenged you and frame it from that position. For example, your understanding of your role's remit might have been challenged. You could say, *'I am finding this difficult because it challenges my understanding of my responsibilities'*, or, using the principles of positive regard and curiosity, *'I am finding this challenging. I know there will be reasons so I am curious to know how it has come about?'*

RESPONDING

WHEN YOU DON'T KNOW WHAT TO SAY

What do you do when you don't know how to respond? You have been asked a question or heard something and expect yourself to act the part and provide a response. Your brain freezes, you're uncertain what to do. It might be momentary but it can seem like ages.

Often the issue is your own expectations, your belief that you should have the answer. You cannot be all-seeing but you can formulate a good question and good questions promote deeper thinking. Questions can range from:

- Buying time – *'What makes you ask that?'* or *'I need some time to think about it'*
- Asking for clarification – *'What do you need from me at this moment?'*
- Challenging their process whilst not responding to content – *'It's okay for you to be mad, but it's not okay for you to be so critical'*
- Acknowledging new information and developing thinking – *'That is new to me. I am going to have to think about it as I am unsure how to respond. What do you think are the most important aspects?'*

You do not have to act a part and respond as you or others expect. Questions can give you flexibility and help retain control.

SUMMARY

Responding is part of the two-way exchange that is conversation. Responding is often *ad hoc* and improvised in relation to what emerges. Often, you'll follow your standard script, a script based on your perception of your respective roles and status. A script is easy because it is habitual; you can respond without too much thought. The problem with a script is you get the same results.

If you want different results then you need to change the script. You need to listen and respond with purpose. Throughout this chapter the intention has been to offer you ways of doing this. Like any new skill they will initially be unfamiliar and feel contrived. The evidence of their value comes from application, so try summarising, practise clarifying, use open instead of leading questions, and ask *'what'* instead of *'why'*.

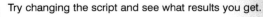

 Try changing the script and see what results you get.

DEVELOPING YOUR LISTENING

OLD HABITS DIE HARD

It is estimated that you run 45% of your life by habit. Habits make everyday routines easier because they require minimal thought and energy. However, encounter a new situation or try to work in a different way and you'll need to think a bit harder. Adapting habits requires deeper thinking, that not only uses a different part of the brain but also consumes more energy, and that is tiresome.

Your listening habits are there to make it easy for you, which is a benefit. Your habits are also deeply ingrained, which is a drawback and:

- When old habits are being challenged you'll feel uncomfortable
- When your new habits aren't strong enough to be familiar the old ones reassert themselves
- The autopilot takes over when a threat arises and the 'fight or flight' response is triggered
- Habits reassert themselves when you are tired and your resolve and energy are low

When strong emotions arise those good listening techniques you've been practising can disappear and push you back into your comfort zone, as in the case on the next page.

THE COMFORT ZONE

Jeff was a manager in a construction related industry where profit margins were low, deadlines tight and penalties high. His success and identity were built on a 'heroic' leadership approach. He was known as a hands on, directive, forceful, problem-solving site manager.

Jeff wanted to become a regional manager and realised his style might limit future success. However, a more participative style of leadership took him out of his comfort zone. In a series of small, low risk experiments Jeff therefore began to develop his style through coaching, using questions and listening to people.

When a major problem arose on site there was pressure to get the site running again and minimise cost. The 'threat' to his role and project caused Jeff's heroic leader style to reappear.

His first imposed solution cost over a £1000 a week in equipment hire. The equipment wasn't up to the problem and malfunctioned. The second imposed solution was too slow and too expensive.

CHANGE OR BUST

Jeff, exasperated, turned to the workforce for ideas. At a brainstorm meeting the solution came from the youngest person on site, an 18 year old. It cost £15 and a morning's work by the site team. Jeff estimated a saving of £30,000 in lost time, equipment hire and potential penalties.

When asked what made it possible, Jeff believed *'I was now in a position to be ready to listen'*.

Old habits die hard. Under pressure and feeling threatened Jeff's old ways had reasserted themselves. Higher order thinking disappeared into a 'fight or flight' response. In this case it was the exhaustion of options that caused Jeff to step back, reflect, think and listen at a higher level. For him the power of a simple solution from the most unexpected place was an epiphany. It accelerated his belief in the changes he was making and his development and he's now a regional manager.

The £15 solution? Fifteen dipping nets from a local pound shop.

DEVELOPING YOUR LISTENING

CHANGE & MOVING FORWARD

As the book closes, here are some key techniques you can use to scaffold your development with structures that support your efforts over the longer term:

- **Awareness** – building self-awareness is the start. Observe yourself and reflect on those observations; seek feedback from others
- **Learning goals** – set yourself meaningful goals with clear reasons/rewards for your effort
- **Marginal gains** – momentum comes from small victories; focus on easy-to-do small changes that move you towards your overall goals
- **Time of day** – when your brain is fresh it is better at higher order thinking; habits reassert when you're tired. Practise new habits when energy is high, ie in the morning
- **Feedback and support** – involve others in your change, ask for their feedback, advice and support (Marshall Goldsmith has excellent work on feedforward)
- **Generosity** – you'll have good days and bad days, like Jeff. Keep your eye on your overall goal, recognise what you're doing well and, above all, be generous to yourself

DEVELOPING YOUR LISTENING

LAST WORD

Listening affects people and organisations day in, day out. Whether it is during times of change or when innovation and creativity are needed, listening plays a vital role. Yet so many people underestimate the effect it can have.

Listening builds trust. It is integral to effective leadership and how we relate to one another. A small everyday action can have a big impact on people's relationships and their motivation towards change, towards innovation, towards you.

If you want to enable change, want greater creativity, want people to engage, then listen a bit harder!

FURTHER INFORMATION

SUGGESTED READING

Here is a select bibliography of work which informs my practice and this book:

Listening and Responding, Sandra D. Collins. Thomson South-Western, 2005

Marshall Goldsmith, www.marshallgoldsmith.com

Swift to Hear, Michael Jacobs. SPCK Publishing, 2000.

The Zen of Listening, Rebecca Z. Shafir. Quest Books, 2003.

For reference, Jane Dutton's research into High Quality Connections is comprehensive and practical.

FEEDBACK Pocketbook

For managers, trainers and team members, a pocketful of techniques to create feedback conversations that underpin learning, build relationships and engage motivation

Mike Pezet